Networking & Local Marketing Strategies
for Wellness Professionals

HOW TO BUILD VALUABLE BUSINESS RELATIONSHIPS
BY CONNECTING WITH YOUR COMMUNITY

Featuring Presentation Transcripts By
Marcus Bird, Andy Ramsay, Gael Wood
& Felicia Brown

Tim Cooper & Gael Wood

Global Wellness Professional Marketing
Summit Success Series

Praise from the readers of "Global Wellness Professionals Marketing Summit Success Series

"In a world gone social media "crazy" with the belief that you need to be seen and attracting clients on the internet to make it big, I found this book so refreshing.

The practical and down to earth ideas about connecting and communicating with my local community and with "real" people provided me with invaluable information and solutions that I can use in my business and in my personal life too."

Karen Stevens
Soul Alignment, Life Upgrades & Transformation

"What I really like about this book is that the marketing and networking information comes from seasoned professionals in the wellness industry. They have actually used the methods they are describing to build success in their businesses. The information is clear, easily actionable, and targeted at wellness professionals."

Dorene Stander, LMT
A Spirited Body, USA

"This book is a wealth of information and valuable advice on how to engage with potential clients and expand your business. The strategies offered make sense and are simple and effective ways for even new business owners to have a positive impact on their client base, sales and business growth. I have found this book to be so beneficial for my business and implementing the different ways of meeting and engaging with people has definitely benefited my confidence to go out and network more freely. Highly recommend this book to all therapists looking to start or grow their business."

Mrs. Justine be Antoska
Naturally Serene Massage Therapy, England, UK

"I enjoyed this book immensely! The Power Pitch was specific and detailed plus I gained a new perspective and knowledge on promoting my business locally. The section about Invite, Inform, Incent will be a game changer.. Thank you to all of the presenters and their expertise and must read for a wellness entrepreneur."

Ann Bell, owner
The Healing Haven
Washingtonville, NY, USA

Tim Cooper Education
1210/10 Fifth Avenue
Palm Beach, Queensland 4221
Australia
https://globalwellnessprofessionalsmarketingsummit.com

Networking & Offline Marketing Strategies for Wellness Professionals / Tim Cooper & Gael Wood —1st ed.

The Global Wellness Professionals Marketing Summit Series

Get the whole series

Success Strategies for Wellness Professionals
Achieve your goals and beat your money blocks

Are you feeling **trapped**, **stuck** and **frustrated** in your business? Feel like you're just **spinning** your wheels? These summit transcripts from Drew Elliott, Daphne Wells, and Rebecca Brumfield will provide you with the tools to get you moving forward again.

Video & Online Marketing Strategies for Wellness Professionals
Unleash the power of video. Stand out, get seen & grow

These summit transcripts from Kevin Anson, Robert Gardner, Tim Cooper, and Delight Iverson will show you the simple steps to using **video** to reach new clients, **build trust** and **authority** and **stand out** from your competition

For more information and links to the Kindle and Paperback editions, please visit

http://gwpms.com/summit-success-series-2018

Preface

With so many different options for marketing your business, it's easy to end up confused or trying to do all-things and doing none of them consistently enough to get real measurable results.

As wellness professionals, we work closely with clients, and it's important to build trust, and confidence in our interactions with them. There's no better way to build trust than an in-person conversation, getting to know our potential clients and letting them know how we can be of service.

That one to one conversation can also be challenging! Where do we find people to talk to and what exactly should we say? It is worth it to put time and effort into finding events to participate in and create a plan. Of course, you could just "wing it," and you will probably get some results, but you might also end up thinking of all the things you "could've/should've" said and done.

A well thought out plan will give you more confidence, and that confidence will influence every interaction that you have.

Whether you are at a business networking event, just out and about, or talking to an existing client about working together, this book will help you to know what to say to promote yourself with confidence.

Congratulations for taking this step and investing your time to learn these invaluable skills.

Gael Wood

Gael Wood
Co-host Global Wellness Professionals Marketing Summit

Foreword

I have been honored to serve the field of massage therapy for the past 20-plus years as editor of *MASSAGE Magazine*. We publish articles on topics including business, research, techniques, news, and self-care—all of which are important, but business is the area that is absolutely crucial for massage therapists to study, understand and apply.

I'm using the term *business* here as an umbrella term that covers marketing, finance, networking, continuing education, retail sales, customer service—and other activities that lead to a successful massage practice and long-lasting career.

Receiving massage and bodywork has changed my life for the better, immeasurably—and it breaks my heart when I hear that many massage therapists don't make it past their third year of practice—sometimes due to physical burnout, occasionally because they lose faith in their ability to run a practice, and oftentimes because they just can't get enough clients onto their table.

The good news is, the problems of burnout, lagging passion and lack of clientele can all be solved by implementing activities to support one's business.

Unfortunately, massage schools don't always have time to include classes on business activities in their curriculum. Schools do a good job of preparing graduates to pass a licensing exam and provide skilled touch, but the responsibility for learning and implementing effective business activities falls on the shoulders of massage therapists—and that's a responsibility that continues throughout the life of the therapist's career.

My emphasis here is on the word *activities*. Business strategies and techniques must be put into practice in order for the therapist to harvest results. These activities must be engaged in on a regular basis. Just as you wouldn't learn a new hands-on technique and not apply it during sessions, learning about effective business techniques and then refusing to implement them might not be the wisest choice for building a successful massage practice.

What do I mean by a successful massage practice? One that is rewarding both in terms of income and the positive results experienced by clients who benefit from the therapist's skilled touch.

As with any reward, stretching oneself—sometimes far outside the usual comfort zone—is necessary to reap rewards. Yet, we human beings aren't always willing to stretch ourselves beyond our comfort zone.

I've had some massage therapists who seem to believe they can hold the key to better health in their hands, yet never really promote their work to potential clients. I've even heard some therapists wonder why, since they have graduated and now know how to give massage, clients aren't seeking them out for sessions. I also frequently hear massage therapists say they would never sell retail; don't see the point in networking; won't be "pushy" by talking about what they offer; can't see themselves using a chair to build business; don't really like computers and so don't have a website; and would never, ever volunteer at a charity or sporting event.

To these therapists I say: No one will know what you offer unless you market your work; burnout will occur unless you engage in passive activities like retail sales; and events are a low-cost way to make the public aware of who you are and how massage might help them.

The successful massage therapists I've known push themselves to learn business skills, keep those skills fresh, and find innovative ways to reach people with their message about healthy touch. They understand the importance of diversification, self-promotion, and networking. This book, "Networking & Offline Marketing Strategies for

Wellness Professionals" effectively conveys exactly how to engage those important activities.

To succeed in the business of massage, therapists must be willing to see themselves in a way that expands on being a massage therapist— as a sales rep, marketer, and networker. It can mean offering products and services for sale, setting up your chair at an event, and being willing to talk about your work to strangers.

However, you are not alone. Thankfully, massage and business experts, including the authors of this book, are here to share their mistakes, advice, and strategies with you, to help you succeed in practice and grow a career that lasts as long as you want it to.

Karen Menehan
Editor in Chief
MASSAGE Magazine

Contents

Networking is more about farming than it is about hunting.

—IVAN MISNER

Introduction

As an introvert, the word 'Networking' chills me to my core. I still have vivid memories of going to meetings and standing in the corner, too shy to speak to anybody. And if anyone approached me for an introduction, I would first have to remove the lather of sweat from my palm before shaking hands.

These days, while I'm not totally paralyzed with fear, I still don't perform well in those environments. And that's fine. Networking events aren't for everyone, but as you'll see, there is much more to networking than attending breakfast meetings.

When setting out to write this introduction, I must admit I was a little stuck. I thought to myself, "Tim, what on earth could you possibly have to say about networking?" Then it hit me. I am extremely good at certain aspects of networking.

While I was totally out of my element at trade shows, breakfast meetings, and similar events, I had built a very successful private practice through networking with medical specialists, medical doctors, physiotherapists, and gym operators. In fact, **approximately 87% of my new clientele came through referrals from my professional network.**

You see, while I was terrified to mingle in a room full of strangers, I had no problems reaching out to strategic partners and forming a mutually beneficial relationship with them.

Then I looked at my time as Head Trainer and Senior Soft Tissue Therapist for the Gold Coast Suns, a national level Australian Rules Football team. Once again, I had to form a relationship with many service providers and suppliers. Soon I found myself the go-to person whenever anyone needed something. I became a **connector**. In no time at all a web of mutually beneficial relationships was built on the back of referring solely within my network.

At certain stages throughout my professional career as a clinical massage therapist, I volunteered my time at **local sports clubs**. While there was no, or little, monetary gain and my involvement did take me away from my clinic, it worked well to raise my profile in the **community.**

I've learned that you receive a lot by giving. Zig Ziglar said, *"You can have everything in life you want if you will just help enough other people get what they want."* I truly believe this.

My community work, while personally gratifying, also resulted in a steady stream of clients to my clinic. Not only did the athletes come and see me, but they also referred their partners, parents, siblings, friends, and work colleagues.

I guess the point I'm trying to make here is the world of networking isn't confined to the naturally outgoing and flamboyant. That even the quiet and reserved amongst us can still benefit greatly from implementing network building strategies and working with the community.

With today's focus on internet marketing and social media platforms, it's easy to get caught up in the creation of automated 'bot' sequences and multimedia messaging. And while we must cater for those who would prefer to communicate with a machine, we must also look beyond technology.

Why is video becoming more and more popular? I believe one of the biggest reasons is that people, now more than ever, are seeking **real connections**. Their B.S. filter is on high alert. Ultimately, people do business with people. And when it comes to consulting and providing treatments you've got to build trust and rapport quickly.

While the internet is a powerful and somewhat required business building tool, the importance of developing networking skills cannot be understated. I know personally, when it came to my private practice, much of my revenue came through my professional network and community work.

The final point I want to make is this. Social networks come and go. *Anyone remember Myspace?* The other issue with online platforms such as Facebook is they keep on changing the rules and place restrictions on what you can and cannot say. It is the opinion of many industry experts that online marketing is only going to become more difficult in the future as platforms and governments respond to privacy issues and other concerns.

At the time of this writing, I'm in the process of establishing a video marketing agency. One of our primary marketing approaches is going to be speaking from the stage, presenting our service offering to a room full of local business owners.

Offline marketing is still a highly effective way to get your services in front of your target market.

One thing you're in total control of is how to interact at a personal 'face-to-face' level. You are in total control of your personal network and community work. That's something that can't be taken away from you. It's an invaluable resource ready to be tapped.

Gael and I hope you enjoy the information as much as we enjoyed compiling it for you. We also hope that you implement the strategies outlined in the book to expand your reach, increase your visibility and build the business of your dreams.

To your success

Tim Cooper

Tim Cooper
Co-host and creator of the Global Wellness Professionals Marketing Summit

Here's Your Free Gift

Exclusive to readers of the Global Wellness Professionals Marketing Summit Success Series.

Working out the best ways to market your business can be challenging to say the least. It's hard to know what really works.

While there are many highly effective free and low-cost strategies to choose from, there are also many options that can end up costing you a lot of time and money.

Without a clear direction, it's 'hope marketing' at best. Without a structured marketing plan, you will find it difficult to know what is actually working and what's not working in your business.

The Affordable Marketing Strategies Discussion Panel

In this 64 minute presentation hosted by Gael Wood, recognized industry experts Felicia Brown, Vicki Marsh, Robert Norberciak and Cath Cox share their real-world experience with what marketing strategies worked best for their specific business model.

You'll discover -

- Simple, **low-cost methods** to get you started. You'll be enlightened and inspired!
- How to grow your business with **zero marketing budget**. No money? Use this instead...
- The best **marketing resources** targetted at our industry

Join us today for this free presentation as wellness industry leaders reveal affordable marketing strategies that work.

Sign up here and get ready to take the headaches out of trying to find new clients without breaking the bank.

Simply click the link below and follow the directions to access the **Affordable Marketing Strategies Panel Discussion** video.

gwpms.com/affordable-marketing

Meet the Speakers

We are extremely honored and grateful to Marcus Bird and Andy Ramsay of Wellness Leadership Academy, Gael Wood and Felicia Brown for their valuable insights and guidance.

The material presented in this book is based on transcripts taken from their contributions to the 2018 Global Wellness Professionals Marketing Summit.

A major challenge we faced while compiling this material is transcripts prepared from live presentations reads very differently to material written specifically for print. Throughout the editing process, we have endeavored to improve the flow of the content without losing the essence of the presentation.

As a result, you will occasionally encounter grammatically incorrect structures and disjointed text. We ask that you look beyond structure and focus on the message. Your persistence will be rewarded.

Marcus Bird & Andy Ramsay
Wellness Leadership Academy

Andy and Marcus have over 30 years combined experience in the Wellness Industry. Both have been successful Wellness Leaders, Clinic Managers, and Online Business Owners.

After collectively working with over 20,000 people globally these guys are considered "the" experts on Wellness Leadership and Integral Education Marketing for the Wellness space...

"Our Mission is to transform the Wellness Industry, one wellness leader at a time. We know when wellness leaders are educated to become heart-centered leaders and build successful businesses, their positive impact grows and the world transforms for the better.

Our job is to freely distribute cutting-edge training and strategies to create authentic wellness leaders and serve up a bigger chunk of the trillion dollar wellness industry profit to those wellness leaders who are on the ground doing the hard work with people in need all over the world."

Gael Wood

Gael Wood is a Massage Therapist and Esthetician with over 22 years of business experience.

She now helps therapists all over the world learn to market their businesses on a budget using content marketing, local networking, and creating marketing materials that attract ideal clients.

She loves to share her enthusiasm for making business promotion fun and creative.

Felicia Brown

Felicia Brown is the owner of Spalutions and provides business and marketing advice to massage, spa and wellness professionals.

She is the author of Free & Easy Ways to Promote Your Massage, Spa & Wellness Business and Creating Lifetime Clients as well as several other books.

Felicia has been a licensed massage therapist since 1994 and owns A to Zen Massage, a wellness spa in Greensboro, NC.

The Power Pitch: How to Share Your Message in 12 Seconds or Less

Marcus Bird:

Hey, there, it's Marcus from the Wellness Leadership Academy. Thanks for tuning in. We really hope you're enjoying this summit. We have a really great training for you today about getting your message out to the world.

One of the biggest problems we find for wellness professionals is answering that dreaded question: What do you do? And what we've found over the years is that, so many times, when people get asked that question, they tend to sort of vomit or throw up on people, because they're so excited. Someone's asked what they do, and they just sort of chuck themselves at people. And what we've found happens is that, when you do that, people step away from you, and you're less likely to get a client or a referral into your business.

So what we've got for you today is one of our core pieces of IP called the Power Pitch, which is all about how to share your message in 12 seconds or less, and lets you get way more new clients and way more referrals. Because one of the key things here is, if you can't share your message in under 12 seconds, if you can't share a clear, concise,

and congruent message, what happens is the impression people are left with is that you can't be very good at what you do.

Now, you and I both know that's *so* not true. But often the message lets you down. So this a really great training that we do and it's taken from one of our live events. I know you're going to absolutely love it.

So often, once people learn these techniques, they get clients *just like that*, time and time again. They get a lot more referrals and have a lot more success. I hope you enjoy the training!

Alright, let's talk about your message. Predominantly, what we want to do right now is we want to help you to answer that horrible, dreaded question that we get asked, which is, "What do you do?" **We want to help you to answer it in a really commercially clever way that's consistent and congruent. It's going to get someone to either step towards you, or away from you.** And either way is fine. What we don't want is people to be half-and-half about us. You want people to love you, or not love you. To like you, or hate you.

In a way, we've got to polarize people, because if we're not polarizing people, we're not going to get anywhere. And one of the biggest issues for most of us in the room is we all want to be liked. Right? So we sit in this gray zone with people, and they don't ever make a decision whether they're really with you, or they're really against you. Especially when you go online, we have to polarize people.

When we do our messaging, that's what we're going to do – we're going to start polarizing people. When you get clear about your niche, you're polarizing people. When you get clear about your egoic label for your A-grade client, you're polarizing people. You're either a corporate executive or you're not. You're either a mom or you're not a mom. You're either looking to conceive or you're not looking to conceive. Instantly, we polarize people, right? Because if we have anyone in the gray zone, nothing's ever going to happen. We're not ever going to get any traction because they never make a decision.

You might be thinking, "Well, it sounds really cool, and I might like to join, but I'm just not really sure." We just drag all these people along with us when we really want, "Yeah, I really love what you do," or "I don't like what you do." Either way is perfect. And so we want to get really clear about that, and we have to do that in our messaging. That's what we're going to do. So most people, when the dreaded question arrives, which is, "What do you do?", they send out this chaotic message that's not congruent, right? And they just, like I said before, verbally diarrhea on people, and just vomit over everybody because they're so excited someone's interested about what they do that they just got to get it all out. Because some of the belief is no one understands natural therapies, people don't really care about it; they don't get it. So I'm just going to vomit as much as I can on someone so that they get it.

And what ends up happening is you keep pushing people away. And you wonder why people aren't running towards you going, "Yes, I have to see you, because you're amazing." You keep pushing people away and we don't want to do that.

We have to send out a really clear and congruent and consistent message. And there are three key things about this when we communicate our message.

The first is we have to share authentically, obviously. **We have to be real about what we're saying.**

The second is we have to do it in under 12 seconds. 12 seconds or less. The latest research shows that when we meet someone for the first time, we tend to make up our first impression of that person in under 12 seconds. There was some research out of NYU in America; they did some research on people who interview people, and how they make their decision on their interviewees. And the shock about it was that they realized that when you go in for an interview, the main impression is made within twelve seconds or less.

The scary part about this, is if you're presenting or meeting a woman, it's 8 seconds or less, and if you're meeting a man, it's 15 seconds. So the average is twelve. Not saying us men are slow or anything, but I just think women are much more connected and therefore go by what they're feeling much quicker.

By the 30-second mark, the impression is done. So they realize that by 30 seconds, the interview decision had already been made and nothing would change it after 30 seconds. So it doesn't matter what happens after 30 seconds if you're going for a job interview, nothing matters. It's the first 12 seconds, and then the 18 seconds or so after that make all the difference, which is a bit scary, right? So all the fluff and all the stuff you vomit on people make no difference after 12 seconds because they're sitting there going, "Nah. I'm not going anywhere near this person."

The third thing is that we've got to make them feel safe. And the key around making people feel safe. To get someone to step toward you, you need to create intrigue; to get people to ask a question. Because the minute someone asks a question, they're giving you permission to share. If they don't ask a question, they're not giving you permission, right? And the question of, "So what do you do?" is not a question of permission. It's a question of politeness. And they don't really care, right? So we've got to craft our message in a way that allows us to do that. **What we've come up with is a process called the power pitch. And we're going to share the power pitch with you right now.**

What we're actually going to do is we're going to get you to do this power pitch. I'm going to explain it to you, and then we're going to fill out the power pitch sheet, and then you're going to run this live. So in about four or five minutes, you're going to run this live, and you're going to see how this plays out.

When we're sharing ourselves with the world, and answering that question, there are three key things that we have to share. We have to share about us, about you. You have to share about "it," which is what you do. Most importantly, you have to share about what's in it for them. These are the three key bits of information you have to get across to someone so that they get a really good feeling about you and they know whether to step forward or to step away. Does that make sense? Great.

So, the standard format for this, when someone says to you, "What do you do?" What do you say? So, most people start with their job, right? So, hi, I'm a doctor, or I'm a lawyer, or I'm a dentist, or a naturopath, or a massage therapist. We start with our job, which actually doesn't tell them anything about us, it tells them about our tool kit, but nothing about us. The biggest issue with that is that if you start with your job, you run the risk of someone dumping you in a big pool of other people with that job.

Hands up if you're a chiropractor. (Marcus sees one person reply.) One. Okay, I'm going to use chiropractor if you don't mind. The method is the same for everybody, but I'll use the example of chiropractor because it polarizes things the best.

So, you get asked, "What do you do?" And you go, "I'm a chiropractor." **You've got three opportunities to engage someone** because everyone's had one of three experiences with a chiropractor. **And this example is for any method, modality, or methodology.**

The first experience is, "I love my chiropractor. I've got a chiropractor, I love my chiropractor. The best thing since sliced bread. Just love my chiropractor." So they're not going to want to really engage with you because they love their chiropractor and why would they change? They wouldn't. Right?

The second experience is, "Oh, yeah, I went to a chiropractor once. I really hurt my neck. Nope, never doing it again." So they're not going to come and engage with you, right?

And the third group are the people who don't know anything about chiropractors. They're the ones who are likely to go, "Oh, tell me about chiropractors." They step toward you, and that's what we want. But this is a pretty small group, right?

Say you get lucky and someone says, "Wow, tell me about chiropractic. I really don't know anything about it." You can go on a talk about what chiropractic is, and that's lovely. But then what happens is you get to the end, they're now interested and they go, "Yeah, I'm really interested in coming to see you. This is cool." But now you get the dreaded question, "How much do you charge?"

So, just as an exercise, what's the lowest you've ever had a chiropractor charge? Someone just yell out a number. How much?

Audience: Fifty.

Marcus Bird: Fifty? Have we got anything lower than fifty?

Audience: Forty.

Marcus Bird: Forty. Great. What's the highest someone's ever heard a chiropractor charge? How much? 120? Have we got any advances on 120?

Audience: 300.

Marcus Bird:

Thank you. 300, sold to the man in the front here. So, 300, right? Now, if we get there and I say, "Wow, this sounds great. It sounds just like what I need, what do you charge?" And my mindset sits here, and you're actually here, what's going to happen? Ooh, I'm going to get sticker shock, right? Or I'm going to get that, sort of feeling of, "Oh, my God, really?" Because I'm not expecting that price.

However, if we don't go out like that, and actually go out with our expertise, lead with our expertise – keep our tool kit just here, but lead with our expertise – what ends up happening, generally, is we create a little pool all of our own!

So, if I go out as a wellness leadership guru or wellness leadership expert, or wellness leadership specialist, how many other wellness leadership specialists have you heard of? None. Right? None. Maybe one other down the back there, Andy. But you haven't really heard of any, right? **So I bypass all this and there's much greater chance someone's going to say, "Oh, what's that?"** Right? Then, when I get down to the dreaded question, if we get that far of this: What does a wellness leadership expert charge? Whatever he wants, right? Pretty much, because there's no benchmark here!

Now, obviously, everyone has their own belief around what's expensive and what's cheap. But you've got a much better chance of capturing someone... well, not capturing someone, but having someone step towards you because that's what we're trying to do. We're trying to get people to step towards us.

So, what we want to do is change this up the scenario. We want to lead with our expertise first, not what we do. Not our job! Because that's not who you are, is it? Just because you're a naturopath, doesn't mean you're actually a naturopath. That's just the job you do. It's a tool kit. You're actually a human being with amazing wisdom and a whole lot of beautiful stuff.

So what we want to start with here — and we're going to run this 12 second pitch here — is your expertise. And this revolves around the problem and the niche that Andy was talking about before. I'm going to get Andy to run his power pitch in a minute so you can see how this works. But we want to start with an expert. So, I'm a fatigue expert. Or I'm the fertility expert. Or I'm the... whatever type of expert.

Now, if your association doesn't allow you to identify as an expert or a specialist, what you revert to is "I have a special interest in..." Okay? So if you can't say "I'm a fertility expert" because associations won't allow you, you say, "I have a special interest in fertility." So far, we believe, and all the research we've done says we're allowed to do that.

So, you want to lead with that – with an expertise around your niche. Once you've lead with that, what you can do then is go and start to share your category. Which is... it could be as a naturopath. I'm going to tell you the segue way words in a minute, but it could be as a naturopath **or** chiropractor. What we would recommend you use here is a wellness consultant, a wellness coach, or a wellness leader, as opposed to identifying with your modality again, because they'll put you in a pool of stuff.

There will be time to share your tool kit if they step towards you. But we don't want to burn them before they've even had a chance to ask you a question, right?

The next thing is your category. And probably the most important part is this part here, because at the end of the day, what people really care about is, "What's in it for me?" Right? So this is where the egoic label comes in. "I help executive women." Or, "I help stressed-out executives." Or, "I do these three things, and these are the benefits."

I'm going to get Andy to share his in a minute, so you can see this. **We want to come up with three core benefits that they get from working**

with you. Which is sort of those pleasure island words that we've done before. And then the final thing we're going to do is we come up to this box and we're going to talk about — and I'll just flip these through so you can actually see it just in case you can't see this — we're going to look at what's the real core benefit they get. So this one here is benefits. And come up with three of those, and then the core benefit. Right? Ben-eh-fit. Which is one thing they get? What's the one core benefit?

So, Andy, can you come up and share yours? And then we're going to work through this for a minute, and then we're going to do it live. So, can you share your 12-second pitch in about 15-20 seconds or so? To be slower? So they can hear what you're saying. All right?

Andy: Yup.

Marcus Bird: So, Andy, what do you do?

Andy:
So, I'm Andy. I'm a wellness leadership expert. And I mentor and train wellness entrepreneurs to help them have more time freedom, location freedom, and financial freedom. And what I'm most passionate about is helping them make a bigger difference on the planet.

Marcus Bird: Right. How was that? Do you want him to do it again?

Audience: Do it again!

Marcus Bird: Okay. Do it again.

Andy:
I'm Andy. I'm a wellness leadership expert. And I mentor and train wellness entrepreneurs to help them have more time freedom, location freedom, and financial freedom. And what I'm really passionate about is helping them make a bigger difference on the planet.

Marcus Bird: Nice work. Round of applause. Thank you, Andy. Okay, so what I want you to do is to go to page 34, and we're going to fill this page out.

Andy: One thing I just want to mention here, is that, what was the last thing I said? Make a bigger difference on the planet.

Marcus Bird: Yeah.

Andy: Who wants to make a bigger difference on the planet?

Marcus Bird: Right.

Andy:

Right? **Because the last thing that you say has to hit the nail on the head. The thing that you're most passionate about has to be the ultimate benefit that your audience wants by working with you.** Does that make sense? So you guys want to make a bigger difference on the planet. That's why I've got that as the very last thing I said, because **that's actually the thing I want you to remember the most.** You could forget all of this, as long as you remember that, because that's all about you. And at the end of the day, you don't really care about me that much.

Marcus Bird: No.

Andy: You want to know whether I can help you.

Marcus Bird: Yeah.

Andy: That's about it, right?

Marcus Bird:

Yeah. Great. So, let's go do this. At the top, we've got what my target market is, and we've talked about the niche and the one person stuff, then what you're going to do is write your name in, "Hi, my name is..."

When people get nervous and anxious, when they share a message, sometimes I've seen people forget their name. So, put your name in so we don't forget that. Then we're going to go fill out "I'm a..." I'm a something. Expert, guru, queen, diva, or have a special interest in. Some people can hold some of these bigger words. So, Andy, when he shares his, says, "I'm a wellness leadership expert." When I do it, I go, "wellness leadership guru."

Because I can hold the word "guru." I'm comfortable with it; I love how it disrupts people's thinking a bit. I love how it makes people squirm a bit. Love that, right? But Andy, not so much. And that's fine. There's no right or wrong. So if you can hold a bigger word, then I would recommend you try that. Because it's going to draw a little bit more attention; it's going to create more intrigue.

So put that down. You're an expert, guru, queen, diva, or whatever. Then "As a..." And this is the category, "As a...wellness consultant; wellness leader; wellness coach." Or, for this exercise if you want to put naturopath, or massage therapist, or whatever your modality is, you can do that, but we would highly recommend you try and move away from that. Okay? But right now if you need to do it, just do it, it's fine.

Andy: Remember that the reason for that is we want you to create your own pool of people.

Marcus Bird: That's right.

Andy:

Your own thing. It's your thing, and you're creating the language around it. So if you then say naturopath, or massage therapist, immediately they're going to put you into another box that they have created.

Marcus Bird: And we don't want to do that.

Andy: Right, you want to create the box for them.

Marcus Bird: Exactly.

Andy: You can't avoid the box, but you can actually create it for them.

Marcus Bird: What a classic!

Andy: They're going to put you in some box.

Marcus Bird: This is hilarious.

Andy: Yeah?

Marcus Bird: I used to talk about that, now you're finishing. It's great. It's great.

Andy: This is what Curoz said to us, remember?

Marcus Bird:

I know. He did. Yeah. So, anyway, we just had a private chat to ourselves for a minute. So then what you want to do is "I help..." And this is where you insert the egoic label. I help women wanting to conceive, or... whatever.

Andy: Professional women.

Marcus Bird: Professional women, or...

Andy: Executive men.

Marcus Bird: Stressed-out executives, or...

Andy: Moms and dads.

Marcus Bird:

Right. So this is where the egoic label goes. "I help..." Did you get that? Great. Then you go help them get these three benefits. One, two three. Then "But what I'm really passionate about is..." is the final statement.

Andy: The benefits are your pleasure island that you did earlier.

Marcus Bird: Yeah. You can just put those in there.

Andy: Yeah.

Marcus Bird: Right. And then, but what I'm really passionate about is this. So, what we're going to do right now...

Andy:

The last thing is the core benefit. The actual thing that they *really, really* want. After those three ... When they're living on pleasure island, what's the ultimate transformation they've got going on? The thing that they're most passionate about?

Marcus Bird:

Great. So what we want you to do now is we're going to give you half a song to complete this. Once we have done the song, we are going to run this with someone we don't know. So you have to have something written down. Don't care whether it's perfect or right or the best thing you've ever done. So, perfectionists, let go. Take a deep breath. It's okay. Procrastinators, take a deep breath, write something! Because you're going to do this live in a minute and there's nothing more embarrassing that standing there and not having anything to say. Right? So it doesn't matter the quality right now. What matters is getting this down fast. Is that clear?

Audience: Yep.

Marcus Bird: What matters most?
Audience: Getting it done!
Marcus Bird: Sorry, what matters most?
Audience: Getting it done!
Marcus Bird:

About five people left in the room. Come on, everybody. What's most important? Get it down fast. Thank you. All right, you've got a song. Ready, set, go. If you need help, once you've had a go, put your hand up and we'll help you out.

So the fun part about this is you wrote this in under a song. Or in a song. And it wasn't necessarily perfect or the best thing you've ever done in your life, but it had a response. And that's all that matters. Imagine if you now have time to just re-tweak it and do it even better, imagine the response you're going to get.

Andy: The ultimate thing you want from that 12-second pitch is intrigue.
Marcus Bird: Yeah.
Andy: All you want, actually, you don't need to worry about anything else. If they feel intrigued by what you've just said...
Marcus Bird: They'll step towards you.
Andy:

Right! They're going to actually step towards you. That's all you want out of it. That's why it's so quick, it's only 12 seconds. Just state your expertise – I'll just say I'm a wellness leadership expert – and then shut up. And then everybody I've said that to will step towards me and they'll ask me about it. "Oh, I've never heard of that, what is that?"

Marcus Bird: Okay. So is that helpful?
Audience (quietly):   Yes.
Marcus Bird: Okay, that doesn't sound right. Is that helpful?
Audience (loudly):   Yes!
Marcus Bird:

Great. So I want to see some of you – all of you – networking, talking to the person who had their hand up. We're going to finish shortly. I just want to help finish off these boxes for you. There's a whole lot of boxes that we didn't fill out. And so, generally what happens when we run this – when you run your 12-second pitch in a normal environment – what you're going to do is stop when you get here. And don't say anything else, unless someone asks you a question. If they don't ask you a question, they're not in your niche, they're not interested, so shut up! Don't vomit on them, because that's just rude. Okay?

If they don't ask you a question after stopping here, they're not interested. So don't waste your breath. Just talk to them. Just go and be social.

So, what are some of the questions that might come off the back of this? What were some of the questions maybe you had after that experience? Just give me an idea. What sort of questions, like, "How do you do that?" How do you do that? Yeah, great. "How do you do that?" What's another question might come up?

Audience: What can they expect...?

Marcus Bird:
What can they expect when they see you? Excellent! What else? Money? Yep. Potentially, yep. What else? "Where are you located?" Could be another one, yep. "How did you get into this field?" There's a number of questions. So what these other boxes do is they complete and answer about 90% of the questions you're going to be asked. And **if you have all of this scripted out and you know this backwards, when someone asks you a question you just reel it off like that.**

What that says to someone is you know what you're doing. You're clear about what you're doing. You've thought about it, you're intelligent, you're smart. I have to come and see you. When you muddle and mumble and bumble around, people will go, I'm not coming to see you because you obviously have no idea what you're doing! Which is not true; it's just the impression they get.

So let's just go through and have a look at some of these others. So let's start down here, because down here is all about detail. So these are detailed people who will ask these questions. And the big-picture people will ask these questions. And we're just generalizing... big-picture, detailed people will ask these type of questions.

So, detailed people might start with things like history. And the classic question around that is "How did you get into the field?" Or, "How did you get into that?" Right? And each of these boxes answer the box above. Right? Or the middle row of boxes. So history answers "How you became an expert in..." or have a special interest in that thing. And **when you talk about history, you want to talk from three places. You want to talk about something that happened a long time ago. Something that happened between now and then. And something that you've been working on the last few years, that's why you became this.**

So as a fatigue expert, I might say, fifteen years ago I was a corporate Jedi and I got chronic fatigue syndrome. Eight years ago, I learned how to heal myself. I became a practitioner and learned a whole lot of really great techniques, and in the last couple of years, I've been helping corporate executives... – the egoic label – I've been helping corporate executives overcome fatigue.

What I'm really passionate about is this. Always end here. So you deliver these three things. So this is something of a long time ago. And really, it's a bit of the Hero's Journey. And it answers how you became an expert. So... fifteen years ago... it doesn't matter. "Fifteen years ago, corporate Jedi got chronic fatigue syndrome. Ten years ago I learned how to heal myself, became a kinesiologist, and learned a whole lot of tools and techniques to overcome fatigue. And in the last couple of years, I've been specializing in helping corporate executives overcome fatigue. What I'm really passionate about is this."

Make sense? The next sort of detail question is often **example.** This is what happens when I come and work with you. And here we just **be very straightforward and specific and systematized.** So if you're in a clinical environment, what you say is, "What happens is this: people come in for an initial session, I do a whole lot of tests, and I do a report of findings. After that, we develop a treatment protocol for you." It could be as simple as that.

Or, "I have a program called the Wellness Journey" – which you've just developed, called this a journey – and what it really is about, "What happens is: people come in, they come in for an initial session, and we then do three sessions online. They come back in and we check what's going on. Then we do another session, then there's another three sessions online, and it's a twelve-week journey." So you explain your wellness journey here. And just give them the detail, the bare-bones detail. Don't go into too much detail, like don't go crazy deep. But just enough that they get what you're about and what's going to happen.

Because really, this question is about, "Oh, my God, when I walk into your room, are you going to push me over, or put needles into me, or do something weird and crazy", right? It's a safety question, the example question.

The next one might be about **results.** "What sort of results do you get?" And there's two ways to answer this. If you're allowed to answer this, then you give a case study. "Well, actually, I was working with a woman exactly like you. She was a corporative executive, and really, really stressed. She used to work for Microsoft. Over a period of 90 days, I helped her to do these three things, and now she's doing this and it's really amazing."

What I'm really passionate about is this. Right?

If you work with men and women, have a male and a female case study. If you can't use case studies because of your registration, then you generalize about the modality. Chiropractors have been known to do this. So, it's general. It's not the best way to do it, but sometimes that's just what you have to do. So if you're playing chiropractor or naturopath or one of the modalities that's AHPRA registered or association registered, then you're not allowed to do testimonials or case studies, so you need to generalize about the methodology. Does that make sense? Okay. So how it helps women get pregnant is this way...

So that's the three bottom ones. The three top ones, again, are for big-picture people. Big-picture people love imagery. So what they're going to want is things like metaphors. Metaphors and analogies. So what you want to do is come up with a metaphor for your expertise, and an analogy for your category. Because, remember, these boxes down here answer these boxes in here. So the results are results that you get here.

So, for the three positives that they get, you've got to have examples of how that happens. So these are the metaphors and analogies. So, **for example,** if I went out as a wellness coach, the analogy of coaching's a little bit like being an air traffic controller. I can't fly your business from A to B, but what I can do is help you to have less turbulence, avoid getting hijacked, avoid going off-course, and to get to where you want to go in a way that is much, much quicker than you can probably do on your own. **That's a bit of an analogy for coaching.**

You want to come up with an analogy for your expertise. And so fatigue might be around things like power station or something like that. And as a kinesiologist, you can play the game of, you know, what I do is help connect the wires together so the energy can flow, so that you can have more abundance of energy, and connect to that internal energy that you've got. Something like that. Does that make sense?

And that'll be based on the question. So, a big-picture person asks things like, "Oh, what's that like?" So, here, as a metaphor about you, you start with, "I'm like..." Dot, dot, dot. And as an analogy for your category, it starts with, "It's like..." So the questions of, "Oh, what's that like?" or "What's that about?" or "How does that work?" is often a big-picture question. And that's how you answer it.

Now, the fun part about this is this power pitch, or message matrix, as we call it, can be used for many different things. It can be used in a radio interview or a podcast interview. So have it in front of you, because they're going to ask you questions around all of these things. You can give it to the interviewer to start with and say, "Hey, here are some questions and answers that I often get asked." You can do that.

The other thing we can use this for – and we'll fill in these numbers – **is the About You page on your website.** Who's got an About You page on their website? Hands up! Great. So most About You pages on your website are chaotic, right? And they ramble on about blah, blah, blah, stuff, right? And there's no system to it. **So we're going to give you a system right now for your About You page.** Is that all right?

Audience: Yeah.

Marcus Bird: Yep. We're going to run over time by a few minutes. Is that okay?

Audience: Yeah.

Marcus Bird:

Right. So here goes. The red numbers were your power pitch. Your 12-second pitch; one, two, three, and four. The gray numbers are how you deliver this on your About You page. And I'm just going to go slowly, but I want you to listen to this. We start with history. We start with ten years ago, this happened. Five years ago, I had this miraculous change, and in the last couple of years I've been focusing on this. That's why I'm an expert in this.

Andy: Your history's basically the Hero's Journey.

Marcus Bird: It is.

Andy:

Joseph Campbell writes about. It's in all great movies, in Hollywood. It's basically your "from woe to win" story. The story that people can relate to, that your A-grade clients can relate to. It has to be relevant.

Marcus Bird:

So, you start with your history. Ten years ago, five years ago, in the last couple years, that's why I'm an expert in this. As an expert in this, I'm a bit like that. I'm a bit like a power station, I'm a bit like an air traffic controller. Whatever. When people come to work with me, this is how it works. We have X amount of sessions, and it works like this. This is the framework of how it works.

As a naturopath, it's a bit like this. As a wellness consultant, it's like this. As a wellness coach, it's a bit like being an air traffic controller. The sort of results I'm getting is this. Male, female. Female, female. Or you go into the story about chiropractic or naturopathy and how it benefits and some of the things that people have experienced, without being specific.

When people work with me, these are the three key benefits they get, but what I'm really passionate about is the top one. So, what we're doing is we're always finishing with what I'm most passionate

about. **What lights me up the most**. Not what gets me most excited. Don't do that one. Do what I'm most passionate about. What lights me up the most. Always finish with that because that's the main thing to remember.

Andy: And it's the thing that they want the most.
Marcus Bird: It is.
Andy:
Remember, you want to make a bigger difference on the planet. So that's what I say. I say, **"I'm most passionate to help practitioners make a bigger difference on the planet,"** or something like that. It happens to be what I'm most passionate about, too.

Marcus Bird: Yeah, so don't lie about it.
Andy: You just got to make sure it's congruent with what you're really passionate about. **But it's got to end with the benefit for them.**
Marcus Bird: Yeah. Does this make sense? Is that helpful?
Audience: Yes.
Marcus Bird: Okay, try again. Is that helpful?
Audience: Yes!
Marcus Bird: Great. I know it's the end of the day.
Andy:
Wait. I want to say something, Marcus.

I've done a lot of business training, and a lot of work in leadership, and Marcus's expertise around his communication and communicating through this model is freaking incredible. I've done a lot of travel, lots of events, and lots of trainings. Nobody has put it together like this, anywhere that I've come across. It is genius, guys. So please, make the most of this. We're giving it to you in this event. Just so that you get your shit together, get your message clear, and get out there and do your work on the planet. This is gold, so please take note of it and implement it.

Is everyone going to implement it?

Audience: Yes.

Andy: Yes?

Audience: Yes!!!

Marcus Bird: Good. We're going to give you a challenge, because your message is part of your future. If you get this right, you'll have an abundance of people coming to see you...

Andy: Absolutely.

Marcus Bird: ...regardless of what you're actually selling. So we're going to give you a challenge. And the challenge is that we want you to embed this straightaway, Okay? So here's the challenge...

Andy: We'll bring that other slide up later again, for you. No, it's not in the book.

Marcus Bird:

Those who are the most courageous, what we want you to do is find someone you don't know tonight, and share that message matrix. That power pitch. Just the 12 seconds. It could be someone at a checkout, someone who can't escape. Just share it, okay? Just deliver it. If you're courageous enough, find someone you don't know and deliver it to them.

We'll give you the second level for those maybe not quite as courageous. Do it to a partner or a friend. Ring a friend or someone and say, "Hey, I just learned this technique, could I try it on you?" And just do it. Deliver it. Because the more you do it now, the more you'll start to embed it, Okay?

And the final way, if you don't have a partner or you can't speak to a friend, if you've got a dog or a mirror, just do it in front of that. All right?

So, who's up for the challenge? Yeah, great. So please go out and do this as fast as possible. Because it'll help to embed the teaching and it'll help you to just get there and keep using it. So please do that. You can then refine it.

Andy: Let's do that real quick.

Marcus Bird: Go.

[TIME LAPSE]

Hey, there, Marcus Bird back with you again. I hope you enjoyed that training. One of the things that we would really encourage is that you go out and use the system as fast as possible. Just so you can start to embed it. Obviously, you're not going to learn it by rote straightaway. But, in time, you will.

Make sure you have power pitches for every niche that you're in, or every expertise you have. I know a lot of you are multi-talented, and so it's okay to have multiple power pitches. But, really, we want you to go and use them. And we have a lot more training in store for you. We've got a really amazing online training that we'd like to gift to you for watching our training in the summit today.

If you click the link below, you can get access to a free training that we run. It runs for about an hour and a half. It is really amazing training that goes much, much more in-depth about how you can become a wellness leader, how you can start to attract more clients, start to generate and leverage an automated income, and eventually get time, location, and financial freedom.

One of the things we want for all of you is to become leaders in the industry. And so this training is going to help you to do that, and help all of us to move the world to wellness.

If you would like to learn more, join Andy and Marcus for more online training at wellnessleadershipacademy.com/online-training/

Enjoying this book so far? We'd love it for you to share your thoughts and post a quick review on Amazon!

Please leave a review at gwpms.com/nsp-review

Attending Local Events to Promote Your Business

Hi and welcome to *Marketing Your Wellness Business at Networking Events*. This is one of my favorite topics to talk about because I feel like it's something that a lot of wellness professionals could get involved in and it would really help their businesses.

A lot of times we don't get involved in bigger events because we just don't quite know what to do when we get there. So, I'm Gael Wood, and I'm very excited that you're reading this chapter. I'm just going to share some strategies with you today and go over the basics of finding networking events and doing a great job participating in them.

You'll find a link to my website at the end of this chapter. I'm also offering some free marketing content and an email marketing class that you can download. So make sure to check that out.

Now, a little about me. I'm Gael, I'm a massage therapist, and I have been a massage therapist for 23 years. I'm also an esthetician. I've owned several different kinds of massage businesses including an out-call business, a therapeutic massage center, a day spa, and I've also worked in many different locations, from resorts to day spas to even doing a lot of chair massage.

I did that at different businesses in town and at different camps and locations like that. I really enjoyed the marketing part of the business as much or more than the massage part.

I just fell in love with marketing because I think it's so fun, and it's just so amazing to turn your actions into clients and money and to be able to work for ourselves, help people, support our families. I'm very passionate about talking to people about marketing. I also love to create marketing content. I have a lot of fun doing that for my content clients. I have an online program called the **Massage and Spa Success Academy** that has recently re-launched. If you head over to my website, you can get on the list to hear more about that.

Why should you go to events and represent your business? Most of us, I believe, have limited thinking. We think, "Oh, well, if I go to an event and I set up a table about myself, I'll meet potential clients." **But that's only one reason to go to events**. The other reason is to meet the other people that are set up at the event, and this is huge. It's one of the main reasons that you should participate in networking events.

You should be looking for **cross-promotion** opportunities as you meet those other business owners and you get to learn about their businesses. How could you and that business owner work together, promote your businesses together? How could you, perhaps, help their employees?

So you always want to be thinking with each person that you meet, what's the next step and the next step. Really, for both of you, because the more you help other people, the more it will help your business. If you can think of a way to help another business owner get the word out about their business, they will do the same for you.

You should also be looking to find new groups to get involved in, and even more events to attend. As you're meeting people at events, you might find out about other networking groups in your area that you can get involved with and help build goodwill in your community. For example, if you're involved in school fundraising events or things like that, people are going to know that Gael from Natural Healing Day Spa, supports the community and comes out to community events. They know that you paid to be there and that your money for your table or your booth went to support their kids and to support the community. So that's another great reason to get out there and get involved.

I've split the types of events that I'm going to cover into two different categories. We've got **business-to-business** events, and then we've got the **community** events.

A business-to-business event would be, for example, your local Chamber of Commerce business expo, and we'll get into more details on different kinds of events like that. I'm not saying that the general public won't attend at all, but it is a business event that you're doing for a business group.

A community event might be more like a fundraiser or a race or something at a school, something at a community center, where it's just going to have a completely different feel to it. I think that it's good to be involved in both types of events.

Some examples of business events would be like I said earlier, the business expos, health fairs. Some of these events are set up as money makers for the event coordinators, or they're just part of the yearly events for that networking group. You don't always have to be a part of the networking group to participate in the event. You would generally if the local Chamber is doing a business expo, you'll get a discount if you're a Chamber member, but pretty much, any business can participate.

Business sponsored health fairs; this could be something like your local hospital might have a health fair for their employees, a school system might have a health fair for their employees. That's something to look into and see what kind of events are available in your area for you to participate in.

Some towns have women's shows. Sometimes those are set up in the mall or a convention center by the expos, home builders' expos. There might be gardening events.

Just do some research and try to find out what kind of events are coming up in your area. You would want at least a few weeks to get ready to do that event so you can really do a good job and make the most of it so that it will promote your business. We'll talk about exactly what you need to take to events, and we'll talk about exactly what you should do once you get there to ensure your efforts help grow your business.

Community events, I would consider that to be more like your local seasonal festivals that you might have. I know in my area, we have pet day, a fall festival, a herbal day. We have a thing where people race wooly worms. We have all kinds of stuff. I would consider that to be more of a community event.

A lot of towns have summer concerts. They might have downtown events. For example, we have an art walk and some different events that happen downtown. Different races that might be fundraisers for things or walkathons, things like that. School career days, local parades, and then your school festivals. A lot of schools have a spring festival, a fall festival, and they're doing all kinds of carnival games. A lot of them have an area where community resources can set up and also where local vendors and local businesses can set up. Those are usually very affordable.

To set up and promote your business at an event can cost you anywhere from nothing to $400 or $500 to have a table for the day. If you start looking into events and the ones that you're looking into are too expensive for you, then I would say, keep looking. Just try to find ones where they're looking at you being there as adding to their program. That might be a health fair for the school system or something like that. I don't think they would charge you at all because they want their employees to know what resources are in the community. Really, if their employees know about massage therapy and they're getting regular massage, that's just going to benefit them. They're going to miss work less; they're going to probably cost less on their health insurance. Different events are going to have different purposes and different costs associated with them.

How can you find events to participate in? Definitely through any networking groups that you already participate in, or just searching online for networking groups in your area. If they have a website, they probably have their events for the year listed. That's where I would start. You might have to do a little digging because quite often, these networking group websites are just set up by volunteers. They might not be optimized for Google, so you might have to search for a couple of different search terms and even go a few pages deep into Google because they've just set up a simple website, and it might not show up on the first page.

Your local papers and magazines will have events in them, and they should have a website or contact information about the event. Even if it's coming up fairly soon, it can't hurt to call and ask about how to get involved in that event. Maybe it's too late for that year, but you could get put on the list for the next year. I would definitely look into any opportunities you see that you might want to be involved in.

Through schools, if you have children in the local school system, if you know people that work with the local school system, that's a good resource. Also, the school websites would have information on different events that are coming up. You could even simply call the schools. You could call your local high school and ask if they have a career day in the spring. Then let them know that you're interested in coming to that and sharing.

Then, of course, through friends, through your family members, through your church, you might find out about some different events. You always want to keep your ears perked up and keep an ongoing list of opportunities that you might want to get involved in.

Another thing you'll want to do is think outside the box. There might be events held by various organizations where members can benefit from your services. My husband is a rock climber, we spend a lot of time at the rock climbing gym, and they have a lot of events. They have competitions; they have different parties and fundraisers. They always want a massage therapist there.

You might find events through your hobbies or your interests. An example could be a camp I visited, it's thousand-acre nature preserve. A few times a year, they have special events for the community to come down there and to be involved and to see the camp. That would be a perfect way to meet a lot of local people that have similar interests to me and who might be interested in wellness.

Things like that will really help you to have an inside connection to things that other people might not think of. Think about the things that you like to do and you might be able to participate in some events that are directly involved with that.

I know that my husband was just saying to me this morning that he got a great job from somebody from the rock climbing gym. They just got to talking. The guy is building a house, my husband's an electrician, and so that was just some natural networking that happened there.

That's just anything that you're involved in. If you go to an exercise class if you work out at a local gym. I know our local YMCA has a healthy Halloween and that would be another great place to set up. You just always want to be thinking of how you can get out there and how you can network.

Once you find an event you want to participate in, what do you need to bring with you? And what should you do when you get there to ensure you make the most of being at that event?

This is where a lot of people struggle. They don't know what to do, or they drop the ball and then feel like, "Well, that was a bust. I didn't book any appointments." But there's so much more to it than just getting that new client or booking that appointment. It's all about the connections that we make.

I'm going to go over with you in detail about what you need to bring and what you should do when you get there. You want to have a very professional looking setup so you can make the most of your event.

This first section is for your table. Depending on what kind of event it is, you might need to bring your own table. I would figure that out first off. If you're paying for an event, quite often, the organizers will provide you with a table, a tablecloth, two chairs, electricity, but it's definitely something that you want to look into and find out. If you need to bring your own table, you can grab a folding table at Wal-Mart for about $50. That is something that you should definitely have in your business supplies. You might need chairs.

Then you want to think about what your table's going to look like. You want to think about if somebody's walking around an area and they're looking at different displays and different tables, what's going to look inviting? What's going to catch their eye?

The first thing I would say is, you want to **have height to your displays**. You don't want to have everything just laying flat on the table. People won't know that there's something they should check out "way over there" if they can't see it. I recommend investing in a couple of information boards that you can find at any office supply store. You know, they're kind of tall, the sides fold, and then you can put really nice pictures of your services, pictures of your business. That's going to be something eye-catching. You could possibly fit two display stands depending on the size of your table. If you want to spend a little more and get a little fancier, you can order some standup banners and other promotional signage from Vistaprint.

You definitely want to have something that's going to let people from a bit of a distance away see the name of your business and see some pictures of what you do so they'll start to be interested in what you have to offer. I always like to try to make my table look nice with some flowers. You just want to make it look inviting, and you want to have stuff at different levels.

I always **have something to give away. Little water bottles are great. A big bowl of chocolate** is my favorite thing to bring to an event because if you have a big bowl of chocolate, everybody at the event will come by your table and talk to you. Because they can't just come by and grab chocolate. They're going to have to visit with you. You can get to know them. You can talk to them, ask them questions. You definitely want to have something like that on your table.

The next thing you want to make sure you have is your marketing materials. Your brochures, maybe some printed copies of your newsletter if you don't have a brochure. You can make a flyer. Don't overthink it. Just bring something that has your services on it, that has a little bit about what you do, how you help people, what kind of conditions that people might have that you can help. So they'll know if they're in the right place talking to the right person.

You want to have your **business cards**. If you sell products, you could bring some **product samples**. You might want to have some coupons or something to give out, to help people take action and book with you. **A coupon that expires within a month is going to encourage somebody to take action a lot more than just a business card**. It doesn't have to be a big discount. It could be a few extra minutes. It could be an add-on or something like that.

You want to bring your **appointment book**, just in case somebody does want to book right then and there. Or your computer with your appointment booking software on it.

You might want to bring some gift certificates, and I would highly encourage you to do some kind of giveaway, even if it's a 30-minute massage or a little gift basket. **Because one of the main things you want to do at a networking event is collect people's contact information.** You want those email addresses so you can follow up with them. Very, very important.

A few more things that you might want to think about. You might want to bring somebody with you to help you with your table in case you need a break, in case you need to go eat something. Or, if you're really shy like I tend to be, it can be good to just have somebody there with you so you can say, "Hey, let's go over there and talk to those people at that booth." You won't have go and do everything by yourself. Even if you don't have a helper, it's definitely the time to get outside of your comfort zone.

Depending on the setup and what kind of event it is, you might want to bring some **music**. You might want to bring an **aromatherapy diffuser** or **massage chair**. I think some events lend themselves more to doing chair massage than others. I don't think that free chair massage is an important part of doing events, if you're a massage therapist. I actually think **it can take away from you being able to meet as many people as possible**. It can take away from your networking opportunities if you get stuck there doing chair massage all day. So unless you have a team of people and you can rotate out who's doing a chair massage, I really don't recommend that. I recommend that you try to, **promote the fact that you do chair massage and get paying customers for that**.

You will want to bring your **credit card processing** if you're going to bring gift certificates or you might have some special offer if people book with you at the event and prepay.

You'll want to bring some **food and water** for yourself in case you do get tied up talking to people all day, which would be a great problem to have. You don't want to be getting tired and grumpy and hungry.

Now you know what to bring and what your setup should be. This is just as important as what you should do when you get to the event. I see a lot of people at networking events just setting up their table waiting for something to happen and waiting for somebody to come by. That's fine because you will meet some people that way. But there is a lot more you can do.

I challenge myself at any networking event that I go to, to try to meet everybody there. What I suggest you do if you're set up in an exhibit hall, in a hotel, the school gym, the school walkway, wherever you are, I would walk around, and I would try to meet everybody else who's also set up. Those are going to be some of your best clients, the people that own businesses, who need to stay healthy and get massages and wellness treatments more than other entrepreneurs. Right?

Try to meet as many people as possible. That can be the other vendors, that can be the people running the event, and then also the people attending the event. Instead of just meeting the people that are attending the event, we're going to extend our reach to everyone involved. Right?

You want to **collect as many email addresses and/or business cards as you can**. I would have a little form for people to fill out. Not everybody has a business card. Also, collect business cards from people for your giveaway or your drawing. **On those business cards or**

entry slips, I would try to write down anything that I talk to that person about that I might want to follow up on later. If they were telling you about how much their husband needs a massage, that's something you're going to want to remember for when you do your follow-ups. If they're telling you how much their feet hurt or their neck hurts, that's something you want to remember so that you can do a good job with your follow-up and not just do generic follow-ups.

Have something to sell. I often hear that somebody went to an event and didn't feel like it was a success, but they didn't really have something specific to sell.

I've made this mistake at events myself. If it's close to a holiday, you could try to actively sell gift certificates or you could run some kind of in-event special that they can only get if they buy it right then. It's just an additional thing you can do, but if you don't have anything specific to sell, I wouldn't be disappointed that you didn't make any sales.

You want to make sure that you're having fun because if you're having fun, more people are going to want to come talk to you, more people are going to want to interact with you, and get to know who you are and what you do. You can even have fun with your giveaway items.

Think about what kind of event you're doing and what would be appropriate for that event. Because the sky is the limit with what you can do. If you're doing a summer concert in the park or something like that, you could give out little bobbles for the children. If you're going to be someplace outside where maybe a lot of people are walking their dogs you might want to have dog treats at your table. Get creative with what you do. **You don't want to just be the same as everyone else.**

Then also, as you're meeting people, as you're collecting names, business cards, things like that, think of how you might be able to help that person or collaborate with that person. That's something else you can write on that business card to follow up on in the next week or so.

That should be your goal for going to an event. It's definitely not like a set up your table and sit there all day kind of a thing. You're really going to need to get out there. That could be hard for us introverts, but I promise you can do it. If I can do it, you can do it. You might just have to plan a day of recovery afterward, right? If you know your energy levels will be depleted and your tolerance for that kind of stuff is low. But I would just make sure you manage that and don't use it as an excuse.

After the event, you want to **have a really good follow-up plan**. Follow up with each person that you met. If you have something specific that you wrote down, then send an individual email or a text or even call them and talk to them.

If you collected a lot of entries to a giveaway or something like that, without a lot of specific information, then you could add those people to your mailing list and do just one email that goes out to everybody. But the most beneficial thing you can do is to follow up with each person as specifically and as individually as possible, because that's going to make them feel really special that you were listening to them, that you cared about their problems and that you really want to help them.

Whether you're following up about collaborating in the future or you're following up about, getting them in for services with you, be as specific as possible.

If you're following up with them about collaborating or networking, try to get that going instead of just being general. Don't just say "Hey, I would love to work with you on that press promotion that we talked about sometime." Say, "I'd love to work with you on that cross-promotion we were discussing. Do you have time to have lunch or coffee next week? I'm free Wednesday and Thursday until 1:00." Let them know that you're serious and that you want to meet up with them and follow through. That's going to have a bigger impact, the more specific you can follow up and actually following up.

I think a lot of people go to events, they do their giveaway drawing, maybe they add people to their mailing list, and that's the most follow-up that they do. We're going to do a lot more than that and really get the most out of events that we go to.

Now, with that being said, trying different events is how you're going to figure out which ones are going to work for you and which ones are going to work for your business. Not every event is going to be a huge hit or a big winner. My recommendations for be to **try several different types of events until you can find the kind that you like to do and then do a few a year**. If you get out and do some races and it's not really your thing, try a business expo. Just try something else. It just depends on what kind of services you provide and who your ideal client is.

I want to invite you over to my website, GaelWood.com, to my resources page where you can check out my marketing content samples. Those are really nice because there's content in there that you can use to create your handouts, to create your flyers. There are images that you can use to create your information boards that I spoke about earlier, photos that you can print. There's a lot of really helpful marketing content there for you. I know that's one thing that can hold us up when we need to create an info-board, it can seem like a big project. What do I put on it? Where do I find the pictures? Having those resources ready for you will help you to get over that procrastination hump.

In the content clubs, I have images, done for you articles, pre-written ad copy, articles that you can share on social media, and plain images that you can use in your advertising. Grab your samples so that you can see everything that's in there. I also have an email marketing class that will help you with your follow-ups. I hope that you'll check that out as well. I hope you got some great ideas for doing some local events in your area. One of these most important things you can do to promote your business is to get out of the office and meet people.

I know one of my coaching clients this week was telling me that she's been to two networking events in the past few weeks. She's met a bank manager who wants chair massage, a lawyer who's interested also in chair massage, the owner of a gym, and she has also signed up at the gym to get healthier, so that was a great side effect of getting out and meeting people. Plus, they're going to do some cross-promoting and some collaborating, and now she's in a Facebook group for local business owners where she can promote her services.

When you get out of your office, one thing leads to another leads to another, and that's how you can grow a local business.

I hope that you got some great ideas. I'm very excited to be sharing these strategies with you because as we help you learn to get out there and market your businesses, you're going to be helping more clients. They're going to be feeling better, and then what are they going to do? That is the ripple effect, and anyway, it's amazing. It's very exciting, and I'm just grateful that you joined me and I'm grateful to be a part of this event. I hope you have a wonderful day!

Once again to learn more about Gael and get your content club samples please visit GaelWood.com

Invite, Inform, Incent

Hi there. It's Felicia Brown with Spalutions, and I want to thank you for joining me today as a part of the 2018 Global Wellness Professionals Marketing Summit. It's a joy to be here with you and I want to thank especially our hosts, Gael and Tim for inviting me to participate this year. Before we get started, I want to just divulge some personal information here and that is that using this system that is a video and screen share for my PowerPoint at the same time is new for me, so if I stumble along a little bit, please bear with me. It's great to be able to learn something new as a presenter while I'm sharing something new with you, the student. So, thanks for your patience and again, thanks for being here.

Now, some of you watching may know me and others may not. So, I want to just share a little personal background with you about myself while I tell you about this class. Today's class is actually entitled Inform, Invite, Incent: Three steps for success in your spa or wellness business. It's a formula that I use quite often in my own practice and business. To tell you just a little bit about the class, the formula INFORM - INVITE - INCENT should be something that helps you in all areas of your business. This is a marketing summit, but I really want you to think about how else you can use this. Not just with your customers but also with your staff, and I'll give you some examples of that as we go along.

If you don't have staff right now, that's okay. You may have them at some later time and you could even think about this as a formula to use with business associates that you're hoping to make a deal with because that's marketing too. So, to tell you a little bit about myself, I've been a massage therapist actually since 1994. In that time, I've also been an owner or partner in several day spas. The first one I started in 1996 and it was just my solo practice. When I sold it in 2005, I had 50 employees and sales of close to $2 million a year. The things that I teach in my classes are the exact same things that I used in my practice and spa to grow it to the level that it went to as well as in my current business.

Right now, I have a wellness spa in Greensboro, North Carolina. By using the same things that I teach, it's grown from a practice of one person, me, to I think we now have a staff of almost 30. I was just counting yesterday or the day before. I believe we have 19 massage therapists on our team as well as several other allied professionals. We have a yoga instructor, we have an esthetician, an acupuncturist and someone that does permanent makeup as well as our whole support team. So, regardless of the discipline that you're in, these strategies can work for you as they worked for me.

I also like to just point out that in with all the success that I've had, I have had failure too. The second spa that I had went through a very difficult time. We were only open for less than a year because I opened right before the economy crashed. I say that to you not for any other reason other than I want you to know that I've seen all sides of business and that's one thing that makes me a really good coach and educator is that I get it. I haven't just been successful all the time. I've had some rough spots too, believe me, plenty of them. I want you to know you're not alone in that if you're going through some tough times.

Just know that I understand that side of it too and I want you to feel comfortable working with me, whether it's just on this class or other things in the future. The last thing I'll tell you about is that I'm a business and marketing coach. Obviously, that's kind of what I do in these classes and I've written several books, two of which are really geared towards massage spa and wellness professionals. That would **be Free and Easy Ways to Promote Your Massage Spa and Wellness**

Business as well as **Creating Lifetime Clients**. You'll have a chance to find out how you can get one of those books for free in just a moment.

The time that we have together today is pretty brief and I want you to know that you may want to talk with me further about what we're doing or what we're talking about today. If you want more information, I want to suggest to you that you think about getting together for a one on one coaching session after the class and if you decide to sign up for that, which you can do at my website that's down below - it's spalutions.com/summit. If you decide you want to do that, you'll get a free copy of my book **Free and Easy Ways to Promote Your Massage Spa and Wellness Business**. I think you'll find that it's very helpful.

It's not a rocket science type of book. It's very digestible. Everything in it is short and sweet. Kind of like this class will be. I think you'll find that it will help you get what you need to do to get your business rolling. So, anyway without further ado, I'll just jump into the material and see where we go. One thing I like to invite people to do in every class is to take action. If you don't get anything else out of this class, here's one of my number one tips in marketing all the time. That is to take action now.

So, here are some things that you can do to take action right now even if you have to leave and can't finish the rest of the class. You can connect with me on Facebook, connect with the summit or feel free to tweet, text, comment, or post about this class and the summit. You may thing, "Oh, well that's just promoting you, Felicia," or, "That's just promoting the summit," but honestly if you share information with your clients like "oh my gosh, I'm taking this great continuing education!" it actually helps them have more faith in you as a practitioner because they see you're trying to be better all the time. It's not just about seeing the client.

So, don't be afraid to promote the fact that you're out there learning. It really is important. Besides that, we'd love to connect with you. So, please connect with me and the summit on Facebook, Instagram, wherever you might happen to find us. So, something I alluded to just a minute or two ago was that marketing isn't just about promoting yourself to clients. I think really there is an important definition of marketing that we all need to think about. Those of us in the hands on or services businesses. That is anything that touches a client and makes them want to do business with you or your company is marketing. So, you may have previously thought about marketing as, "Oh, I'm sending out postcards for people's birthdays or I'm passing out business cards at the networking event."

That is definitely marketing, but I want you to begin thinking about *every* interaction that you have with someone - including the time you have your hands on them - as a part of your marketing. I also want you to think about things that make a positive or negative impression such as a clean bathroom or a dirty trashcan as something that is sending a message to your client about whether they want to do business with you or not. Honestly people are getting so much information all the time now, positive and negative about really from everywhere. When they come into your business, you want every single impression that they have of you to be positive so that they're reassured that they've made the right choice, that they choose to come back. Don't just think that it's all going to be dependent upon how good your work is. Because that's just a small piece of it.

So, change this definition of marketing in your head. It will probably change your outlook about everything you listen to in this whole summit. I also want to get clear on what "doing business with" means. When I say "doing business", really we're talking about someone getting a service, making a purchase, sending you a referral, etc. You could think of doing business also as making sales. I kind of laugh when I say that out loud because I know especially in the massage world, when you say the word sales, people get this deer in the headlights look and they're like oh my gosh, I don't want to do sales, right? I don't know. It's a scary word I guess is what I would say.

So, I'm here to tell you, it's okay. Selling our services is kind of how we make a living. I want you to just try to get comfortable with those terms doing business and making sales because the reality is we're all doing it every day. So, I want to talk about that "doing business" as an important facet of this class because in order to be profitable, in order to pay our bills and make money and achieve the goals we have set in our wellness or massage or spa business, we have to continually look for ways to do more business. Really, it boils down to this.

I learned this from a client actually at a conference years ago. I thought it was just so succinct and well put. There's only really three ways to do more business or to get more sales in your business. One of them is to add more new clients. That's pretty obvious and as a coach, I get more requests for, "Felicia, can you teach me how to get more new clients?" than anything else.

The second thing and second way to get more business or to do more business is to retain those new clients and to get them to come in more often or again. In fact, if you just think about if you're able to get every single new client to come in just one more time, you can really double the amount of business you're getting from each person. If you have a lot of "one and done" type people, then there's possibly some problems in your system and that's another issue, but getting people to come back is really one of the biggest secrets of success and longevity in business no matter what field you're in.

Then the third way to do more business is to increase your sales to each client at each visit. There's a lot of different ways to do that, but those are the top three things. So, add more new clients, retain new clients and get them to come back and then increase the sales at every single visit. Now, why do we want to increase sales? Well, of course we're in business. We have to make a living and hopefully we are making a better living the longer we are in business.

So, number one we're doing this to maximize our revenue per client, but the second reason that we want to increase our sales is the more important one. That is **to enhance the value that each client gets from each visit to your business.** I want to just put it in perspective. I teach classes on rebooking all the time. I don't have time to go into all the details of it, but I want you to just think about the difference of going to see someone for, let's say, acupuncture and you go and you see them for one visit. Maybe it helps a little bit and you get decent results, but then you move and you have to go to a new town and see somebody else.

So, you have to go through the whole getting to know you process all over again. You have to fill out the paperwork. You have to get comfortable with it. You have to learn where their bathroom is and how they do business. You get one acupuncture session and then you have a good result and then boom, you have to move to another town. You have to start the process all over again. So, even though sequential acupuncture visits might be doing you some good. Imagine if you were able to stay with the first practitioner that you felt good with and you were able to build a rapport and a trust and a relationship where they got to know you.

Because of getting to know you, not only were they doing a better job each time, but they were able to provide you with recommendations for other things that you might like or refer you to other practitioners and that trust allowed you to relax more into the treatment. So, you can see that if you build a relationship with people and you're in to really enhance the value that the client is getting at every visit much differently than if someone was going to a different practitioner every single time. Hopefully that makes sense. When you see the correlation between increasing sales to a specific client versus just getting them on time, then this INFORM - INVITE - INCENT strategy might make a little more sense too.

So, thinking about selling. A lot of people in our industry, particularly in the massage world where I live, don't want to sell. They feel very uncomfortable with it and they'll give you all kind of reasons why they don't want to sell. So, for example, they think it's being pushy or salesy and they don't like that. They'll say specifically, "Well I'm a..." fill in the blank. "I'm an esthetician. Not a salesperson." Perhaps their afraid of being rejected or they don't have confidence about what it is that they're selling or recommending. In some cases, if it happens to be about a particular product or service, maybe they don't feel like they know enough about the product or service to sell it effectively.

That's very common. There are some people that don't want to sell because they don't believe in what it is they have to offer. So, if you don't believe in the services that you're providing and believe it or not, there are practitioners out there that are trained in things that they don't like. They have it on their menu but they don't feel confident enough in the service itself to recommend it. So, they won't and they wonder why no one ever gets it. It's kind of humorous. A lot of cases on the product side, practitioners feel that selling a product is somehow unethical. That it doesn't jive with the hands-on care.

I just don't believe that that's true. If you're selling something outside of your scope of practice, for me as a massage therapist, if I were to sell nutritional supplements for an example, I don't have any training in nutrition. I can tell people what I like and what's worked for me, but outside of that, I can't tell them what they need. So, that might be unethical, but for me to sell someone, let's say, some lavender essential oil that I just used in the session they had, I don't think that's unethical at all. You have to be the judge for your own practice, but this is just some of the reasons that people don't sell. I bet some of them sound familiar to you.

I believe the truth is that selling your products and services as well as your business as a whole is helping people solve problems. Let's be honest. People in healing arts that are service providers that give that type of care, we're in it to help people, right? That's the whole point. So, by offering services that we do and by offering products that complement that, we are helping people's problems. We're helping solve people's problems. That's why they come to us. So, it's important to realize that when they have something they're trying to get help with and they're seeking you out as the professional to give them that help, then you've got to have the solutions.

Whether it's for pain relief, health, beauty, overall wellness or whatever. So, just keep that in mind and start thinking about selling as problem solving instead of salesy, okay? I know you can do it. When you have that confidence and the belief in what it is that you're selling, then you are going to have much better results. People will believe in you because you believe in you. They are going to relax into your care. They're going to put their trust in you and they are going to have a better result from everything that you recommend. So, I know that seems like a lot of preview before the INFORM - INVITE - INCENT but I kind of wanted to build up to that so that when you hear this information, you'll be like, "You know what? Okay. I'm ready. I understand why it's important to sell. I'm confident and how here's a new tool I can use. INFORM - INVITE – INCENT. "

INFORM - INVITE – INCENT. It's not something you have to say to anybody or anything. But when you are putting together your promotions and talking to people about things that you think they should try, remember this formula. It will help you have a much better success rate with people. So, let's talk about what these things mean. First of all, looking at inform. So, when we're talking about your clients, information is really just giving people that information. Giving them the knowledge about the products and services that you offer, what the benefits or results are that they're going to get and how that relates to the goals or outcomes that they were seeking. That's pretty much it. So, let's say that a client comes in to you with a headache. So, you're going to think about the list of treatments or products that you have that could help with a headache.

You might say, "Well, Jennifer, as far as my treatments go, I think doing an upper body massage will really help relax some tension in the back and shoulders." I'm just spit balling here so doesn't have to be massage, doesn't have to be Jennifer, but I'm just giving you an example. "So, what I would recommend as treatment for your headache and then as a take home item, I personally really like peppermint oil. I'm going to use some in the massage so that you can see what it's like. Then if you want, we'll talk about how you can take it home at the end of the session." So, you start with the information part and letting them know what this is, how it's going to benefit them and how it's going to help them get the results that they want.

Generally speaking, people are going to make purchases or book appointments, take a referral because of the results that they're going to get. As well as the ease of use or the experience that they have with it and the value. It's important to remember the value doesn't necessarily mean that it's cheap. It's not the same thing as price. Just yesterday as an example, I ended up with an emergency massage client who walked into my spa who's been terrible problems with headaches and back pain and shoulder pain. When she colored in her intake chart, when she colored in the little figure, the whole thing was black.

So, I get her on the table and I'm working with her and I said to her, "You know, I think I'm going to run over a few minutes. Is that okay with you?" I said, "It's my treat. I'm just running over like an extra five minutes or so. I said, "It's my treat, but I just want to make sure that's okay."

What she said to me was, "I don't care. I would pay anything to feel better." Right? So, if someone's feeling bad, there's generally the price isn't as much of an issue as the result. She was right there, so me offering her extra time was an easy upsell. I didn't really have time to do more than that or I would have maybe said, "Let's do a 90 minute session," but running over an extra five minutes was something I could add in for a little extra value on what she was already paying.

So, just think about that and how you can cater to giving people the results or the experience or the value that they're craving. Now, what people are looking for in a service can be different. Here's an example with a couple who come in for a couples' massage and why they might come in. The woman says, "I want this service because I want quality time with my husband. It's like a date and I'll get to relax, plus get to take a nap and it's near my favorite tea shop." She has this whole list of reasons why she's coming in for this couples' massage.

The husband on the other hand says, "I want this service because it's going to make my wife happy. It'll help my neck pain, give me some time away from the kids. They take American Express which means more points, and it's next to the brew pub that I really like."

So, you have to understand a little bit about what the clients are looking for in order to give them the right information. That takes a little bit of exploration if you're looking to try and understand more about clients and what their likes and dislikes are or how to determine your ideal clients, you might want to look at my book **Creating Lifetime Clients**. That was one of the ones I showed you a few minutes ago because it really focuses in on learning who your ideal client is and how to cater to them.

Here's another example about informing clients. "I'm excited to tell you about your new infrared body wrap. Deep heat relieves pain in the joints and muscles like what you have in your knees and hips. You can relax on a massage table and can do it alone or after any service." So, when you're telling people about these services or products that you think they should try, make sure to relate it back to whatever it is that they're there for. Those aches and pains that you know they have or any other needs that might be relevant.

If you're thinking about using inform for your team, it's important to remember we're marketing to our staff just as much as we're marketing to our clients, here's a way that you might inform your team about something that you're trying to accomplish. "Hey, we've set a goal at the clinic to increase overall sales for next month by $2000. If we reach this goal, we'll be able to purchase a new computer for the staff area which will help everyone."

So, getting people information so they understand why they should take part in something, why they should purchase a service or why they should do what needs to be done to accomplish a goal is really helpful in going to want to take a next step, which is responding to your invitation.

With invitations, there's all different kinds of things that you can invite clients to participate in and different ways you can do it. You can provide a free consultation, and inthat consultation, ask if you can recommend services or products to meet their goals and needs. If it's with products, encourage people to try them like with testers or counter cards, samples or using them in the business.

Remember my headache example where I talked with Jennifer, "We're going to use some peppermint oil in your massage so you can try it out." That's a way to invite someone to try it. With services, you can provide brochures, offer videos, articles, demonstrations, many services, or you can just simply ask someone to try it but there's a lot of ways to give people that invitation to take a next step.

Some examples for clients, skincare. "Here's a sample of serum that will help moisturize the dry skin you mentioned. Try it for a few days to see how you like it." If it was in the case of a business maybe or wellness coach, "Would you like to sign up for free mini coaching sessions so you can see what working together would be like?"

So, the invitation is really just trying to get someone to do something. Taking that next step. Not complicated, but it is good to have a plan and to understand what their goals are so you know what to invite them to do or try.

If you're talking about using this formula with your staff, you might say, "John, your goal is to increase your retail sales by $400 in April. If you sell just one $20 cleanser or sunscreen per workday, you'll reach $440 in sales in 30 days. Do you think you can do that?" It's basically just opening the door and telling people how they can take a next step to get to where they want to go. It's a little bit different with staff, but the idea is to start building a pathway so that they actually take part in whatever it is that you're offering.

The final piece of this INCENT. Incentive is really about sharing the love. As a wellness or as a marketing business coach, I find that a lot of times, the incentive part is where people struggle. I want to point out a few things about it. Incentives, first of all, don't have to be discounts. I know depending on your discipline and where you're located, offering discounts or any sort of referral incentive might go against your licensure. So, before you put something like this into practice, it's really important to know that. It's important to have a clear picture of what you can do so that you don't get yourself in trouble. Really important to think about that.

Also, incentives do not mean breaking the bank. So, a lot of times what I see is people that they seem to think that incentive means you have to give away a whole service for free or you have to discount it deeply by 50 or 100% or some crazy number. Then there ends up being a lot of resentment and frustration on the part of the provider. Frankly, that is just too much. So, when you're thinking about incentives or to get someone to try something new or to take the next step and go from single openings into packages or what have you, I really want to stress the point that you as the sales person, the service provider, the one doing the work, you have to feel comfortable with whatever these incentives are. Please do not do something that is going to cost your business too much money or that's going to create resentment in you.

I don't want to create an incentive where every time someone comes in to use it, you roll your eyes, take a deep breath and you're like, "God, another one." That's really not the point. In fact, if you're not feeling good about it, you're not going to give good service and you are kind of shooting yourself in the foot. When I talk about incentives, I really want you to think about how you can make this good for you too.

I'll give you an example before we get any further into this. So, for me, I know that my bottom price for me as a service provider for massage is $65 an hour. It's actually getting ready to go up, but $65 is the least amount of money for a massage. Now, I might give someone a massage for free just because I want to, but I will not charge someone less than $65 for an hour because if I do, that little irritated feeling starts rising up and I don't do a good job. Knowing that that's my bottom level, I have a higher price than that for my top level which is $80. When I get $80 I feel great, but if have an incentive that allows someone to come in and see me for $65, I still feel great. See what I mean?

You have to think about if discounting is one of your planned incentives. You have to create your pricing in such a way that that incentive doesn't make you mad. Your business should be healing for you too. If you're resentful, angry, frustrated, depressed or whatever, when someone comes in to use an incentive, it's not going to be healing for you.

So, just take that for what it is and let's talk about incentives. So, incentives are about sharing the love. Remember like I said, you have to be part of that love too. So, there's a lot of different ways you can create some incentives for people. For clients, this can include things like discounts, specials, a gift with purchase or having some sort of referral program. It might be that you have some sort of guarantee or return program if it's for products or I know some service providers that will guarantee their work like I promise you'll get these results within X amount of days. This might be the case with someone like a plastic surgeon perhaps. Where they have clinical studies of how a machine works or something.

I haven't seen as many of those, but that might be something that you have or in the case of products, obviously a return program is an incentive that might help someone take a step to do something because they're not worried. Some other things that you can do to incentivize clients are simply share before and after photos if you're doing something that creates a visible change in some skin or face or weight. Then that can be an incentive. It doesn't have to be a discount.

Certainly, other incentives out there can be things like testimonials and reviews. We use these quite often in my business when we get a review on a therapist that's particularly good. We'll send it out in a Facebook ad. I'll put the therapist's picture along with the testimonial review wherever it happened to come from, be it Facebook or Yelp or wherever. Then I'll invite people to come in and try that therapist if they haven't seen them before for a special price or percentage off. We'll actually combine those two incentives (testimonial and discount) but you don't necessarily have to.

Incentives, also you can go back to those common benefits and results. If that's just not information, it's incentive because people want those results. Think about what you can do to get people to come and try things out.

I know some therapists and massage therapists or body workers that will provide a free consultation to come in and talk about it. That might be the incentive " Get a free consultation if you book today." Often what the incentive is a take action button. It's whatever is in front of us to take action now. So, book now and get this. You want people to have that incentive so that they decide to come in. It's sort of that push to get them off the ledge so to speak.

With your team, incentives obviously come in a lot of forms, payment being one of them. I really urge anyone that hires people to be really clear about how you pay every service and sale, particularly when it comes to retail sales.

I know I had one consulting client years ago that didn't pay her staff for their retail sales until the end of the year. So, if they sold $1 million worth of products from January to November and were supposed to get $10,000 worth of a bonus, if they left December 1st, they didn't get the bonus. They had to stay through the end of the year to get it. I really thought that was just a bad way to do it because what would incentivize someone if they weren't 100% positive they were going to be rewarded for their hard work? Another way you can incentivize team: offer prizes or bonuses for specific performance. At my first spa, we would have a gift certificate sales contest because we did a lot of gift certificate business. In the summer, we would set a monetary goal like "In December we want to sell $100,000 worth of gift certificates and if we get to that number, everybody's going to get a $100 bonus."

You can do something like that for a group or you can do it for individuals. "Hey whoever meets this benchmark, whoever gets 10 clients to rebook this week, gets free tickets to the movies" or "Whoever sells the most in retail is going to get dinner on me at your favorite restaurant." Doesn't even have to be that much, but whatever it is, having clear incentives be put out there again and again are a big thing.

Of course, just praise and recognize people for their efforts and their results that they get. I think one of the biggest things I do as a boss (and I really try not to be a boss – is that I'm there to be a coach and a guide and a mentor) is I constantly thank people for being there, for doing a good job. When I hear someone get a compliment, when I see them do something well, I just go out of my way to let them know again and again and again how that was great. I really appreciate you.

Know sometimes the best incentive you can give to your clients is to thank them for being your clients. Everybody likes to hear that they did a good job and that you appreciate them. So, that can be one of the best incentives of all. To summarize, and I know this is a lot of information in a short period of time, but I want you to start increasing the use of INFORM – INVITE - INCENT. It's going to help you do more business, both with your clients as well as with your staff. It's going to give you more confidence and you're going to get better results. It's also going to help strengthen the relationships that you have with people and improve stability and revenue for your business overall.

I hope that that's been really clear. I just basically say now, what are you waiting for? This is super easy. Just put it into place. If you want more help, go to spalutions.com/summit. As I said, this is a new technology for me. Right here it says, "Get free goal setting exercises and one on one coaching specials." What that's supposed to say is "Get my free ebook on five tips for rebooking your clients." That's hilarious. So, if you want goal setting exercises too, feel free to let me know. In fact, I'll put them on the page spalutions.com/summit so that you can get them there, but what the real offer is the free ebook on five tips for getting clients to rebook.

So, double bonus for you because of my newbie status with this software and very busy schedule. But I do invite you to go to that website and check things out. If you need some help, if you really feel like you need some help with the one on one side of things, whether it be promotions together with this INFORM – INVITE - INCENT formula, please go to spalutions.com/summit. If you have questions or you just want to learn more about me and what I do, you can go to my website spalutions.com or feel free to email me at felicia@spalutions.com. I'd really love to work from you and hear from you and you'll definitely get access to other goodies when you sign up for the ebook or decide to do coaching.

I do try very hard to provide a super good value for the people that I'm working with because you know you'll get better results if you continue to work with me. So, again that spalutions.com/summit. I just want to thank you for being open minded and taking your practice to a new level by putting this formula in place. If I can be of any other service to you now or in the future, I hope you'll let me know and thank you so much for being a part of this class. For putting up with my little miscues here in learning how to use this software and I do hope that I'll see you somewhere soon. Please come introduce yourself and let me know you saw me here. Thank you for your time. I bless you and your business and wish you much success. Namaste and have a fantastic day.

Meet Your Hosts

Tim Cooper

Tim Cooper is a Remedial Massage Therapist, coach, author, podcaster, and educator.

Before studying massage in 2003, Tim worked as a software design engineer and business analyst for over 20 years.

In 2013 Tim completed his first marketing course and fell in love with the science of marketing and social psychology.

Tim brings a unique blend of industry, technical and business knowledge to his coaching clients and students around the world.

Gael Wood

Gael Wood is a Massage Therapist and Esthetician with over 22 years of business experience.

She now helps therapists all over the world learn to market their businesses on a budget using content marketing, local networking, and creating marketing materials that attract ideal clients.

She loves to share her enthusiasm for making business promotion fun and creative.

Global Wellness Professionals Marketing Summit

Tim and Gael are passionate about the wellness industry and seeing wellness professionals succeed. That's why the Global Wellness Professionals Marketing Summit was born! To help massage therapists, acupuncturists, chiropractors, naturopaths, homeopaths, Reiki healers, energy healers, Bowen therapists, spa owners... everybody involved in the health and wellness industry to prosper.

Right now people are spending three times more on natural health and wellness than conventional medicine. Now is YOUR time to shine. You just need a roadmap, time proven and tested strategies to get you there and keep you there.

Here's your free gift to help get you started!

gwpms.com/affordable-marketing

One Last Thing...

If you enjoyed this book or received value from it in any way, then we'd like to ask you for a favor: would you be kind enough to leave a review for this book on Amazon? It'd be greatly appreciated!

Please leave a review at gwpms.com/nsp-review

www.ingramcontent.com/pod-product-compliance
Lightning Source LLC
Chambersburg PA
CBHW051330220526
45468CB00004B/1575